my gardening
journal & planner

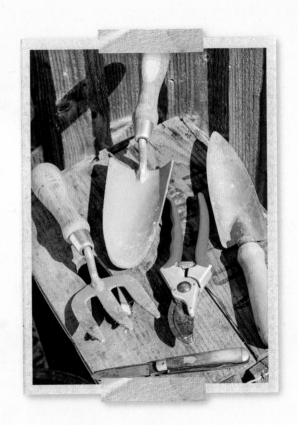

my gardening
journal & planner

CICO BOOKS
LONDON NEW YORK

Published in 2017 by CICO Books
An imprint of Ryland Peters & Small Ltd

20–21 Jockey's Fields
London WC1R 4BW

341 E 116th St
New York, NY 10029

www.rylandpeters.com

10 9 8 7 6 5 4 3 2 1

A CIP catalog record for this book is available from the Library of Congress and the British Library.

ISBN: 978-1-78249-410-2
Printed in China

Designer: Emily Breen
Art director: Sally Powell
Production controller: David Hearn
Publishing manager: Penny Craig
Publisher: Cindy Richards

contents

introduction

The earth is packed with potential, ready to be unlocked with some plants, a few tools, patience, and perseverance.

This journal is an indispensable companion for gardeners. The front of the journal includes grids to plan your personal plot. The journal is then divided in to six sections including Flowering Plants, Trees and Shrubs, Vegetables, Fruits, and Herbs, and each section has record pages to keep track of what you've planted where, germination times, when you planted up, which varieties grew well, harvest or pruning times, and much more.

Also included are pages for Keeping Organized, with space for jotting down favorite websites and stores, as well as a year planner to help you schedule what you need to do when.

With this invaluable record you will not only get the very best from your garden but also have a wonderful resource of your own garden wisdom to refer to for years to come.

planning your plot

Take some time to think about the layout of your plot before you start
planting. Consider factors such as how much space each plant will need,
crop rotation, and the direction of sunlight. Use the grids provided to work
out how you want your garden to be. A careful hour spent deciding what to
plant where will save a lot of time and effort later in the growing process.

9

10

12

14

notes

flowering plants

Every garden needs flowers in some shape or form—whether you choose to cultivate a classic rose garden, fill pots and containers to overflowing with colorful bedding plants, plant up magnificent borders with annuals and perennials, or design window boxes to provide flowers all year round.

When buying annuals or bedding plants, it's very easy to forget which varieties have been successful in your garden, so use the following pages to keep a record of what you have planted. If you like to cultivate colorful displays of springtime bulbs, keep a note of what you have planted where—this will prevent you accidentally digging up bulbs that have started to grow.

From zingy nasturtiums to colorful aquilegias and delicate honesty, many flowers produce copious amounts of seed. Once the seedheads have developed, you can either leave them for the wind to scatter the seed around your garden or you can pick the seedheads, place them in a paper bag, and leave them to dry out. Store the seeds that drop from the dried seedheads in envelopes labeled with the plant name, and you will be ready to grow your own flowers from seed the following year. When growing from seed, keep a record of how long the seeds take to germinate and resist the temptation to plant out seedlings until any danger of overnight frost has passed. And if you find that all your seedlings have grown on and you have more than you need, swap plants with other keen gardeners to extend the range of flowers in your garden.

annuals

Flower name:

Variety planted:

Seeds sown:

Germination period:

Seedlings planted out:

Location:

Comments:

Flower name:

Variety planted:

Seeds sown:

Germination period:

Seedlings planted out:

Location:

Comments:

Flower name:

Variety planted:

Seeds sown:

Germination period:

Seedlings planted out:

Location:

Comments:

Flower name:

Variety planted:

Seeds sown:

Germination period:

Seedlings planted out:

Location:

Comments:

Flower name:

Variety planted:

Seeds sown:

Germination period:

Seedlings planted out:

Location:

Comments:

Flower name:

Variety planted:

Seeds sown:

Germination period:

Seedlings planted out:

Location:

Comments:

Flower name:

Variety planted:

Seeds sown:

Germination period:

Seedlings planted out:

Location:

Comments:

Flower name:

Variety planted:

Seeds sown:

Germination period:

Seedlings planted out:

Location:

Comments:

Flower name:

Variety planted:

Seeds sown:

Germination period:

Seedlings planted out:

Location:

Comments:

Flower name:

Variety planted:

Seeds sown:

Germination period:

Seedlings planted out:

Location:

Comments:

Flower name:

Variety planted:

Seeds sown:

Germination period:

Seedlings planted out:

Location:

Comments:

Flower name:

Variety planted:

Seeds sown:

Germination period:

Seedlings planted out:

Location:

Comments:

Flower name:

Variety planted:

Seeds sown:

Germination period:

Seedlings planted out:

Location:

Comments:

Flower name:

Variety planted:

Seeds sown:

Germination period:

Seedlings planted out:

Location:

Comments:

Flower name:

Variety planted:

Seeds sown:

Germination period:

Seedlings planted out:

Location:

Comments:

Flower name:

Variety planted:

Seeds sown:

Germination period:

Seedlings planted out:

Location:

Comments:

Flower name:

Variety planted:

Seeds sown:

Germination period:

Seedlings planted out:

Location:

Comments:

Flower name:

Variety planted:

Seeds sown:

Germination period:

Seedlings planted out:

Location:

Comments:

Flower name:

Variety planted:

Seeds sown:

Germination period:

Seedlings planted out:

Location:

Comments:

Flower name:

Variety planted:

Seeds sown:

Germination period:

Seedlings planted out:

Location:

Comments:

Flower name:

Variety planted:

Seeds sown:

Germination period:

Seedlings planted out:

Location:

Comments:

perennials

Flower name:
....

Variety planted:
....

Seeds sown:
....

Germination period:
....

Seedlings planted out:
....

Location:
....

Comments:
....
....
....
....
....
....
....
....

Flower name:
....

Variety planted:
....

Seeds sown:
....

Germination period:
....

Seedlings planted out:
....

Location:
....

Comments:
....
....
....
....
....
....
....
....

Flower name:

Variety planted:

Seeds sown:

Germination period:

Seedlings planted out:

Location:

Comments:

Flower name:

Variety planted:

Seeds sown:

Germination period:

Seedlings planted out:

Location:

Comments:

Flower name:

Variety planted:

Seeds sown:

Germination period:

Seedlings planted out:

Location:

Comments:

Flower name:

Variety planted:

Seeds sown:

Germination period:

Seedlings planted out:

Location:

Comments:

Flower name:

Variety planted:

Seeds sown:

Germination period:

Seedlings planted out:

Location:

Comments:

Flower name:

Variety planted:

Seeds sown:

Germination period:

Seedlings planted out:

Location:

Comments:

Flower name:

Variety planted:

Seeds sown:

Germination period:

Seedlings planted out:

Location:

Comments:

Flower name:

Variety planted:

Seeds sown:

Germination period:

Seedlings planted out:

Location:

Comments:

Flower name:

Variety planted:

Seeds sown:

Germination period:

Seedlings planted out:

Location:

Comments:

Flower name:

Variety planted:

Seeds sown:

Germination period:

Seedlings planted out:

Location:

Comments:

Flower name:

Variety planted:

Seeds sown:

Germination period:

Seedlings planted out:

Location:

Comments:

Flower name:

Variety planted:

Seeds sown:

Germination period:

Seedlings planted out:

Location:

Comments:

Flower name:

Variety planted:

Seeds sown:

Germination period:

Seedlings planted out:

Location:

Comments:

Flower name:

Variety planted:

Seeds sown:

Germination period:

Seedlings planted out:

Location:

Comments:

Flower name:

Variety planted:

Seeds sown:

Germination period:

Seedlings planted out:

Location:

Comments:

Flower name:

Variety planted:

Seeds sown:

Germination period:

Seedlings planted out:

Location:

Comments:

Flower name:

Variety planted:

Seeds sown:

Germination period:

Seedlings planted out:

Location:

Comments:

Flower name:

Variety planted:

Seeds sown:

Germination period:

Seedlings planted out:

Location:

Comments:

Flower name:

Variety planted:

Seeds sown:

Germination period:

Seedlings planted out:

Location:

Comments:

bulbs

Flower name:
....

Variety planted:
....

Bulbs planted:
....

Germination period:
....

Location:
....

Flowering period:
....

Comments:
....
....
....
....
....
....
....
....

Flower name:
....

Variety planted:
....

Bulbs planted:
....

Germination period:
....

Location:
....

Flowering period:
....

Comments:
....
....
....
....
....
....
....
....

Flower name:

Variety planted:

Bulbs planted:

Germination period:

Location:

Flowering period:

Comments:

Flower name:

Variety planted:

Bulbs planted:

Germination period:

Location:

Flowering period:

Comments:

Flower name:

Variety planted:

Bulbs planted:

Germination period:

Location:

Flowering period:

Comments:

Flower name:

Variety planted:

Bulbs planted:

Germination period:

Location:

Flowering period:

Comments:

Flower name:

Variety planted:

Bulbs planted:

Germination period:

Location:

Flowering period:

Comments:

Flower name:

Variety planted:

Bulbs planted:

Germination period:

Location:

Flowering period:

Comments:

Flower name:

Variety planted:

Bulbs planted:

Germination period:

Location:

Flowering period:

Comments:

Flower name:

Variety planted:

Bulbs planted:

Germination period:

Location:

Flowering period:

Comments:

Flower name:

Variety planted:

Bulbs planted:

Germination period:

Location:

Flowering period:

Comments:

Flower name:

Variety planted:

Bulbs planted:

Germination period:

Location:

Flowering period:

Comments:

Flower name:

Variety planted:

Bulbs planted:

Germination period:

Location:

Flowering period:

Comments:

Flower name:

Variety planted:

Bulbs planted:

Germination period:

Location:

Flowering period:

Comments:

Flower name:

Variety planted:

Bulbs planted:

Germination period:

Location:

Flowering period:

Comments:

Flower name:

Variety planted:

Bulbs planted:

Germination period:

Location:

Flowering period:

Comments:

Flower name:

Variety planted:

Bulbs planted:

Germination period:

Location:

Flowering period:

Comments:

Flower name:

Variety planted:

Bulbs planted:

Germination period:

Location:

Flowering period:

Comments:

Flower name:

Variety planted:

Bulbs planted:

Germination period:

Location:

Flowering period:

Comments:

Flower name:

Variety planted:

Bulbs planted:

Germination period:

Location:

Flowering period:

Comments:

Flower name:

Variety planted:

Bulbs planted:

Germination period:

Location:

Flowering period:

Comments:

notes

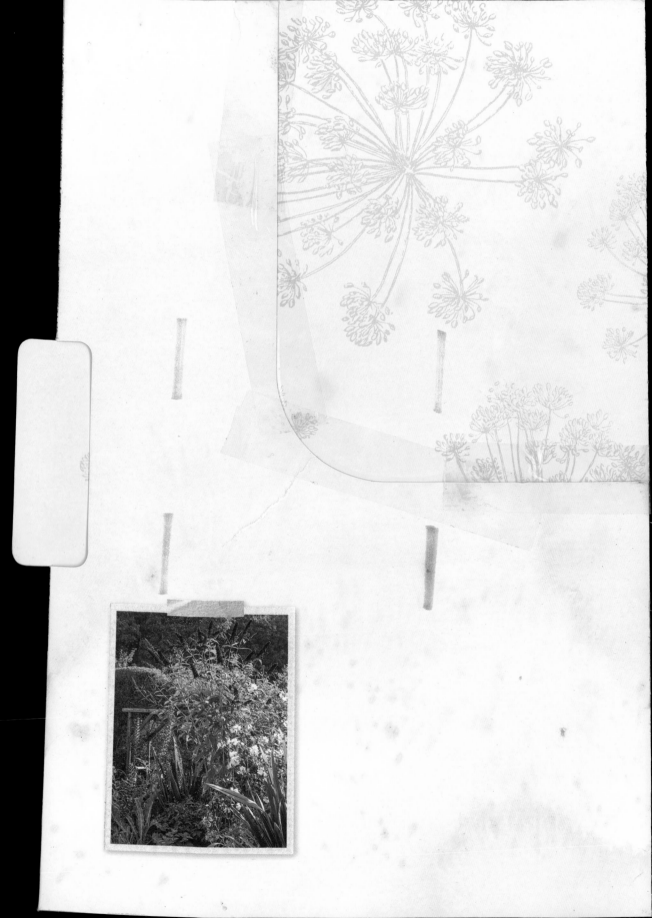

trees and shrubs

For some people, a garden simply isn't complete without trees to give height and shrubs to add interest all year round. When selecting a tree from a nursery or garden center, always check the maximum height it will grow to, and consider whether you want a tree to offer some shade, provide privacy, or add a burst of color with leaves or blossom.

It's just as important to select a tree's planting position in the garden carefully—bear in mind how far roots can travel underground and do not plant too close to the house or other buildings to avoid root damage. Ask advice, too, about how often your chosen tree will need pruning, and the best time of year to do this, and then note down in the following pages the dates that you carry this out. Make sure that you keep the blades of pruning shears and loppers sharp so that you can make clean cuts when pruning.

Shrubs can add structure to beds and borders and if you choose evergreen varieties, they will provide interesting focal points in the garden when other plants have died back in winter. Some varieties even flower during the colder months, making you feel that spring—and warmer weather—is on its way. As with trees, shrubs can benefit from regular trimming to keep them in shape and to encourage new growth.

trees

Tree name: ....

Variety planted: ....

Date planted: ....

Pruning: ....

Comments: ....

....

....

....

....

....

....

....

....

Tree name: ....

Variety planted: ....

Date planted: ....

Pruning: ....

Comments: ....

....

....

....

....

....

....

....

....

Tree name:

Variety planted:

Date planted:

Pruning:

Comments:

Tree name:

Variety planted:

Date planted:

Pruning:

Comments:

Tree name:

Variety planted:

Date planted:

Pruning:

Comments:

Tree name:

Variety planted:

Date planted:

Pruning:

Comments:

Tree name:

Variety planted:

Date planted:

Pruning:

Comments:

Tree name:

Variety planted:

Date planted:

Pruning:

Comments:

Tree name:

Variety planted:

Date planted:

Pruning:

Comments:

Tree name:

Variety planted:

Date planted:

Pruning:

Comments:

Tree name:

Variety planted:

Date planted:

Pruning:

Comments:

Tree name:

Variety planted:

Date planted:

Pruning:

Comments:

Tree:

Variety planted:

Date planted:

Pruning:

Comments:

Tree name:

Variety planted:

Date planted:

Pruning:

Comments:

Tree name:

Variety planted:

Date planted:

Pruning:

Comments:

Tree name:

Variety planted:

Date planted:

Pruning:

Comments:

Tree name:

Variety planted:

Date planted:

Pruning:

Comments:

Tree name:

Variety planted:

Date planted:

Pruning:

Comments:

Tree name:

Variety planted:

Date planted:

Pruning:

Comments:

Tree name:

Variety planted:

Date planted:

Pruning:

Comments:

Tree name:

Variety planted:

Date planted:

Pruning:

Comments:

shrubs

Shrub name:
....

Variety planted:
....
Date planted:
....
Pruning:
....

Comments:
....
....
....
....
....
....
....
....
....

Shrub name:
....

Variety planted:
....
Date planted:
....
Pruning:
....

Comments:
....
....
....
....
....
....
....
....
....

Shrub name:

Variety planted:

Date planted:

Pruning:

Comments:

Shrub name:

Variety planted:

Date planted:

Pruning:

Comments:

Shrub name:

Variety planted:

Date planted:

Pruning:

Comments:

Shrub name:

Variety planted:

Date planted:

Pruning:

Comments:

Shrub name:

Variety planted:

Date planted:

Pruning:

Comments:

Shrub name:

Variety planted:

Date planted:

Pruning:

Comments:

Shrub name:

Variety planted:

Date planted:

Pruning:

Comments:

Shrub name:

Variety planted:

Date planted:

Pruning:

Comments:

Shrub name:

Variety planted:

Date planted:

Pruning:

Comments:

Shrub name:

Variety planted:

Date planted:

Pruning:

Comments:

Shrub name:

Variety planted:

Date planted:

Pruning:

Comments:

Shrub name:
....

Variety planted:
....
Date planted:
....
Pruning:
....

Comments:
....
....
....
....
....
....
....
....

Shrub name:
....

Variety planted:
....
Date planted:
....
Pruning:
....

Comments:
....
....
....
....
....
....
....
....

Shrub name:
....

Variety planted:
....
Date planted:
....
Pruning:
....

Comments:
....
....
....
....
....
....
....
....

Shrub name:
....

Variety planted:
....
Date planted:
....
Pruning:
....

Comments:
....
....
....
....
....
....
....
....

Shrub name:

Variety planted:

Date planted:

Pruning:

Comments:

Shrub name:

Variety planted:

Date planted:

Pruning:

Comments:

Shrub name:

Variety planted:

Date planted:

Pruning:

Comments:

Shrub name:

Variety planted:

Date planted:

Pruning:

Comments:

notes

vegetables

There are five main vegetable groups: root vegetables, salad leaves, brassicas, legumes, and onions. There are also smaller groups that include pumpkins and tomatoes, amongst others.

To successfully grow root vegetables, such as parsnips and radishes, the plants must have a steady source of nutrients in the soil, cool climate, and good drainage. Potatoes are popular and achieve good yields in well-prepared soil, as will carrots and beets (beetroot).

Salad leaves are quick and relatively simple to cultivate. They are shallow-rooting and need regular watering in the evening to stop the compost drying out; prolonged drought stunts the growth of salad plants, producing tough bitter leaves.

Brassicas include cabbages and broccoli. They flourish in cool, moist conditions and suffer if exposed to a lot of direct sunlight. Plant brassicas in the same patch in late fall/autumn—most varieties grow in the same environment.

Legumes include beans of all kinds and are easy to grow. They suffer from few pests or diseases and tolerate most weather conditions. Another advantage is that they are highly nutritious—for some varieties it's best to eat the young green pods, while for others you can leave them on the plant to ripen into beans to be dried for eating in winter.

Plants from the onion family are a good choice for novices as they generally do not need much watering or nutrients. One thing onions do like is sunlight—plant them in a bright spot and weed regularly to avoid blocking out the sun.

root
vegetables

Vegetable name:

Variety planted:

Seeds sown:

Germination period:

Seedlings planted out:

Harvest:

Comments:

Vegetable name:

Variety planted:

Seeds sown:

Germination period:

Seedlings planted out:

Harvest:

Comments:

Vegetable name:

Variety planted:

Seeds sown:

Germination period:

Seedlings planted out:

Harvest:

Comments:

Vegetable name:

Variety planted:

Seeds sown:

Germination period:

Seedlings planted out:

Harvest:

Comments:

Vegetable name:

Variety planted:

Seeds sown:

Germination period:

Seedlings planted out:

Harvest:

Comments:

Vegetable name:

Variety planted:

Seeds sown:

Germination period:

Seedlings planted out:

Harvest:

Comments:

Vegetable name:

Variety planted:

Seeds sown:

Germination period:

Seedlings planted out:

Harvest:

Comments:

Vegetable name:

Variety planted:

Seeds sown:

Germination period:

Seedlings planted out:

Harvest:

Comments:

Vegetable name:

Variety planted:

Seeds sown:

Germination period:

Seedlings planted out:

Harvest:

Comments:

Vegetable name:

Variety planted:

Seeds sown:

Germination period:

Seedlings planted out:

Harvest:

Comments:

Vegetable name:

Variety planted:

Seeds sown:

Germination period:

Seedlings planted out:

Harvest:

Comments:

Vegetable name:

Variety planted:

Seeds sown:

Germination period:

Seedlings planted out:

Harvest:

Comments:

Vegetable name:

Variety planted:

Seeds sown:

Germination period:

Seedlings planted out:

Harvest:

Comments:

salad
leaves

Vegetable name:

Variety planted:

Seeds sown:

Germination period:

Seedlings planted out:

Harvest:

Comments:

Vegetable name:

Variety planted:

Seeds sown:

Germination period:

Seedlings planted out:

Harvest:

Comments:

Vegetable name:

Variety planted:

Seeds sown:

Germination period:

Seedlings planted out:

Harvest:

Comments:

Vegetable name:

Variety planted:

Seeds sown:

Germination period:

Seedlings planted out:

Harvest:

Comments:

Vegetable name:

Variety planted:

Seeds sown:

Germination period:

Seedlings planted out:

Harvest:

Comments:

Vegetable name:

Variety planted:

Seeds sown:

Germination period:

Seedlings planted out:

Harvest:

Comments:

Vegetable name:

Variety planted:

Seeds sown:

Germination period:

Seedlings planted out:

Harvest:

Comments:

Vegetable name:

Variety planted:

Seeds sown:

Germination period:

Seedlings planted out:

Harvest:

Comments:

Vegetable name:

Variety planted:

Seeds sown:

Germination period:

Seedlings planted out:

Harvest:

Comments:

Vegetable name:

Variety planted:

Seeds sown:

Germination period:

Seedlings planted out:

Harvest:

Comments:

Vegetable name:

Variety planted:

Seeds sown:

Germination period:

Seedlings planted out:

Harvest:

Comments:

Vegetable name:

Variety planted:

Seeds sown:

Germination period:

Seedlings planted out:

Harvest:

Comments:

Vegetable name:

Variety planted:

Seeds sown:

Germination period:

Seedlings planted out:

Harvest:

Comments:

onion
family

Vegetable name:

Variety planted:

Seeds sown:

Germination period:

Seedlings planted out:

Harvest:

Comments:

Vegetable name:

Variety planted:

Seeds sown:

Germination period:

Seedlings planted out:

Harvest:

Comments:

Vegetable name:

Variety planted:

Seeds sown:

Germination period:

Seedlings planted out:

Harvest:

Comments:

Vegetable name:

Variety planted:

Seeds sown:

Germination period:

Seedlings planted out:

Harvest:

Comments:

Vegetable name:

Variety planted:

Seeds sown:

Germination period:

Seedlings planted out:

Harvest:

Comments:

Vegetable name:

Variety planted:

Seeds sown:

Germination period:

Seedlings planted out:

Harvest:

Comments:

Vegetable name:

Variety planted:

Seeds sown:

Germination period:

Seedlings planted out:

Harvest:

Comments:

Vegetable name:

Variety planted:

Seeds sown:

Germination period:

Seedlings planted out:

Harvest:

Comments:

Vegetable name:

Variety planted:

Seeds sown:

Germination period:

Seedlings planted out:

Harvest:

Comments:

Vegetable name:

Variety planted:

Seeds sown:

Germination period:

Seedlings planted out:

Harvest:

Comments:

Vegetable name:

Variety planted:

Seeds sown:

Germination period:

Seedlings planted out:

Harvest:

Comments:

Vegetable name:

Variety planted:

Seeds sown:

Germination period:

Seedlings planted out:

Harvest:

Comments:

Vegetable name:

Variety planted:

Seeds sown:

Germination period:

Seedlings planted out:

Harvest:

Comments:

tomatoes

Vegetable name:

Variety planted:

Seeds sown:

Germination period:

Seedlings planted out:

Harvest:

Comments:

Vegetable name:

Variety planted:

Seeds sown:

Germination period:

Seedlings planted out:

Harvest:

Comments:

Vegetable name:

Variety planted:

Seeds sown:

Germination period:

Seedlings planted out:

Harvest:

Comments:

Vegetable name:

Variety planted:

Seeds sown:

Germination period:

Seedlings planted out:

Harvest:

Comments:

Vegetable name:

Variety planted:

Seeds sown:

Germination period:

Seedlings planted out:

Harvest:

Comments:

Vegetable name:

Variety planted:

Seeds sown:

Germination period:

Seedlings planted out:

Harvest:

Comments:

brassicas

Vegetable name:
....

Variety planted:
....
Seeds sown:
....
Germination period:
....
Seedlings planted out:
....
Harvest:
....

Comments:
....
....
....
....
....
....
....
....
....

Vegetable name:
....

Variety planted:
....
Seeds sown:
....
Germination period:
....
Seedlings planted out:
....
Harvest:
....

Comments:
....
....
....
....
....
....
....
....
....

Vegetable name:

Variety planted:

Seeds sown:

Germination period:

Seedlings planted out:

Harvest:

Comments:

Vegetable name:

Variety planted:

Seeds sown:

Germination period:

Seedlings planted out:

Harvest:

Comments:

Vegetable name:

Variety planted:

Seeds sown:

Germination period:

Seedlings planted out:

Harvest:

Comments:

Vegetable name:

Variety planted:

Seeds sown:

Germination period:

Seedlings planted out:

Harvest:

Comments:

Vegetable name:

Variety planted:

Seeds sown:

Germination period:

Seedlings planted out:

Harvest:

Comments:

Vegetable name:

Variety planted:

Seeds sown:

Germination period:

Seedlings planted out:

Harvest:

Comments:

Vegetable name:

Variety planted:

Seeds sown:

Germination period:

Seedlings planted out:

Harvest:

Comments:

Vegetable name:

Variety planted:

Seeds sown:

Germination period:

Seedlings planted out:

Harvest:

Comments:

Vegetable name:

Variety planted:

Seeds sown:

Germination period:

Seedlings planted out:

Harvest:

Comments:

Vegetable name:

Variety planted:

Seeds sown:

Germination period:

Seedlings planted out:

Harvest:

Comments:

Vegetable name:

Variety planted:

Seeds sown:

Germination period:

Seedlings planted out:

Harvest:

Comments:

legumes and other vegetables

Vegetable name:
....

Variety planted:
....

Seeds sown:
....

Germination period:
....

Seedlings planted out:
....

Harvest:
....

Comments:
....
....
....
....
....
....
....
....
....

Vegetable name:
....

Variety planted:
....

Seeds sown:
....

Germination period:
....

Seedlings planted out:
....

Harvest:
....

Comments:
....
....
....
....
....
....
....
....
....

Vegetable name:

Variety planted:

Seeds sown:

Germination period:

Seedlings planted out:

Harvest:

Comments:

Vegetable name:

Variety planted:

Seeds sown:

Germination period:

Seedlings planted out:

Harvest:

Comments:

Vegetable name:

Variety planted:

Seeds sown:

Germination period:

Seedlings planted out:

Harvest:

Comments:

Vegetable name:

Variety planted:

Seeds sown:

Germination period:

Seedlings planted out:

Harvest:

Comments:

Vegetable name:

Variety planted:

Seeds sown:

Germination period:

Seedlings planted out:

Harvest:

Comments:

Vegetable name:

Variety planted:

Seeds sown:

Germination period:

Seedlings planted out:

Harvest:

Comments:

Vegetable name:

Variety planted:

Seeds sown:

Germination period:

Seedlings planted out:

Harvest:

Comments:

Vegetable name:

Variety planted:

Seeds sown:

Germination period:

Seedlings planted out:

Harvest:

Comments:

Vegetable name:

Variety planted:

Seeds sown:

Germination period:

Seedlings planted out:

Harvest:

Comments:

Vegetable name:

Variety planted:

Seeds sown:

Germination period:

Seedlings planted out:

Harvest:

Comments:

Vegetable name:

Variety planted:

Seeds sown:

Germination period:

Seedlings planted out:

Harvest:

Comments:

Vegetable name:

Variety planted:

Seeds sown:

Germination period:

Seedlings planted out:

Harvest:

Comments:

notes

fruits

Even if you have only a small outdoor space, you can still grow some of your own fruit, either on a tree or in plant form. Many fruit-bearing plants grow happily in containers, and some orchard trees have been bred especially for this purpose. As a rule fruits suffer in cold conditions, so protect plants carefully from frost and winds and make sure they are in a position where they receive a decent amount of sunlight.

Grape vines thrive if grown in a warm, sunny place. They need enough soil to retain moisture, and should be pruned regularly to reduce leafy growth and promote a well-formed plant that will yield a fair harvest. A good nursery will advise on the best type of vine for your climate and conditions.

Strawberries are one of the easiest fruits to grow. Both cultivated strawberries and the wild or alpine type need to be kept moist and will tolerate some shade. Allow the berries to ripen fully to a dark red color, and pick them to eat straight from the plant.

Physalis (also called cape gooseberries) are easy to grow and generally not attacked by pests. Seeds germinate quickly, or you can buy young plants. Like tomatoes, to which they are closely related, physalis need warmth and sun to ripen.

All fruit will benefit from a weekly high-potash liquid feed when the fruit begins to mature. A tomato feed is ideal; organic varieties are readily available.

tree fruit

Fruit name:

Variety planted:

Pruning:

Harvest:

Comments:

Fruit name:

Variety planted:

Pruning:

Harvest:

Comments:

Fruit name:

Variety planted:

Pruning:

Harvest:

Comments:

Fruit name:

Variety planted:

Pruning:

Harvest:

Comments:

Fruit name:

Variety planted:

Pruning:

Harvest:

Comments:

Fruit name:

Variety planted:

Pruning:

Harvest:

Comments:

Fruit name:

Variety planted:

Pruning:

Harvest:

Comments:

Fruit name:

Variety planted:

Pruning:

Harvest:

Comments:

Fruit name:

Variety planted:

Pruning:

Harvest:

Comments:

Fruit name:

Variety planted:

Pruning:

Harvest:

Comments:

Fruit name:

Variety planted:

Pruning:

Harvest:

Comments:

Fruit name:

Variety planted:

Pruning:

Harvest:

Comments:

Fruit name:

Variety planted:

Pruning:

Harvest:

Comments:

Fruit name:

Variety planted:

Pruning:

Harvest:

Comments:

Fruit name:

Variety planted:

Pruning:

Harvest:

Comments:

Fruit name:

Variety planted:

Pruning:

Harvest:

Comments:

Fruit name:

Variety planted:

Pruning:

Harvest:

Comments:

Fruit name:

Variety planted:

Pruning:

Harvest:

Comments:

Fruit name:

Variety planted:

Pruning:

Harvest:

Comments:

Fruit name:

Variety planted:

Pruning:

Harvest:

Comments:

Fruit name:

Variety planted:

Pruning:

Harvest:

Comments:

bush fruit

Fruit name:

Variety planted:

Pruning:

Harvest:

Comments:

Fruit name:

Variety planted:

Pruning:

Harvest:

Comments:

Fruit name:

Variety planted:

Pruning:

Harvest:

Comments:

Fruit name:

Variety planted:

Pruning:

Harvest:

Comments:

Fruit name:

Variety planted:

Pruning:

Harvest:

Comments:

Fruit name:

Variety planted:

Pruning:

Harvest:

Comments:

Fruit name:

Variety planted:

Pruning:

Harvest:

Comments:

Fruit name:

Variety planted:

Pruning:

Harvest:

Comments:

Fruit name:

Variety planted:

Pruning:

Harvest:

Comments:

Fruit name:

Variety planted:

Pruning:

Harvest:

Comments:

Fruit name:

Variety planted:
Pruning:
Harvest:

Comments:

Fruit name:

Variety planted:
Pruning:
Harvest:

Comments:

Fruit name:

Variety planted:
Pruning:
Harvest:

Comments:

Fruit name:

Variety planted:

Pruning:

Harvest:

Comments:

Fruit name:

Variety planted:

Pruning:

Harvest:

Comments:

Fruit name:

Variety planted:

Pruning:

Harvest:

Comments:

Fruit name:

Variety planted:

Pruning:

Harvest:

Comments:

Fruit name:
....

Variety planted:
....

Pruning:
....

Harvest:
....

Comments:
....

....

....

....

....

....

....

....

Fruit name:
....

Variety planted:
....

Pruning:
....

Harvest:
....

Comments:
....

....

....

....

....

....

....

....

Fruit name:
....

Variety planted:
....

Pruning:
....

Harvest:
....

Comments:
....

....

....

....

....

....

....

....

Fruit name:
....

Variety planted:
....

Pruning:
....

Harvest:
....

Comments:
....

....

....

....

....

....

....

....

notes

herbs

As long as they have good soil, plenty of light, and a fair amount of sun and warmth, most herbs will thrive. If you are new to vegetable gardening, it is no bad thing to start by growing herbs. You will soon graduate to growing vegetables, and then you can put your herbs and vegetables together in the kitchen and create some delicious meals.

Among hardy perennial herbs that can survive at quite low temperatures are the alliums. This family includes chives, a useful everyday herb that is easy to grow and has pretty purple, edible flowers. Welsh onions are similar to chives but have rather bulbous hollow leaves; and garlic chives have straplike leaves and lovely white flowers.

Sweet marjoram, oregano, and thyme will tolerate dry conditions. Tarragon needs space, but is also worth growing—make sure you choose the French type, it has the best flavor. Rosemary and sage are larger evergreen shrubs with a woody framework and should be planted with a good depth of potting mix. Mint is also popular with gardeners—Korean and American mountain mints are good for making tea.

Annual herbs, which last for one season only, should be grown from seed. Indispensable varieties include basil, dill, and cilantro (coriander). Garden chervil is another annual herb, and is useful for cooking. Annuals will flower and set seed in a season.

herbs

Herb name:

Variety planted:

Seeds sown:

Germination period:

Seedlings planted out:

Comments:

Herb name:

Variety planted:

Seeds sown:

Germination period:

Seedlings planted out:

Comments:

Herb name:

Variety planted:

Seeds sown:

Germination period:

Seedlings planted out:

Comments:

Herb name:

Variety planted:

Seeds sown:

Germination period:

Seedlings planted out:

Comments:

Herb name:

Variety planted:

Seeds sown:

Germination period:

Seedlings planted out:

Comments:

Herb name:

Variety planted:

Seeds sown:

Germination period:

Seedlings planted out:

Comments:

Herb name:

Variety planted:

Seeds sown:

Germination period:

Seedlings planted out:

Comments:

Herb name:

Variety planted:

Seeds sown:

Germination period:

Seedlings planted out:

Comments:

Herb name:

Variety planted:

Seeds sown:

Germination period:

Seedlings planted out:

Comments:

Herb name:

Variety planted:

Seeds sown:

Germination period:

Seedlings planted out:

Comments:

Herb name:

Variety planted:

Seeds sown:

Germination period:

Seedlings planted out:

Comments:

Herb name:

Variety planted:

Seeds sown:

Germination period:

Seedlings planted out:

Comments:

Herb name:

Variety planted:

Seeds sown:

Germination period:

Seedlings planted out:

Comments:

Herb name:

Variety planted:

Seeds sown:

Germination period:

Seedlings planted out:

Comments:

Herb name:

Variety planted:

Seeds sown:

Germination period:

Seedlings planted out:

Comments:

Herb name:

Variety planted:

Seeds sown:

Germination period:

Seedlings planted out:

Comments:

Herb name:

Variety planted:

Seeds sown:

Germination period:

Seedlings planted out:

Comments:

Herb name:

Variety planted:
Seeds sown:
Germination period:
Seedlings planted out:
Comments:

Herb name:

Variety planted:
Seeds sown:
Germination period:
Seedlings planted out:
Comments:

Herb name:

Variety planted:
Seeds sown:
Germination period:
Seedlings planted out:
Comments:

Herb name:

Variety planted:
Seeds sown:
Germination period:
Seedlings planted out:
Comments:

notes

keeping organized

Maintaining and nurturing your garden requires a degree of organization and this section provides a handy year planner with plenty of space to record important monthly or weekly tasks to be carried out over your garden's year. Here, you can keep a log of when you have performed simple tasks such as pruning, trimming, and tidying your garden. Crucial information on pests and diseases that have attacked your plants can be recorded alongside information on which treatments have been successful. Kitchen gardeners can keep notes of when to sow and harvest bounty, crop rotations, and the best companion plantings. There's also plenty of space for contact details of favorite nurseries and websites.

Whether it's scheduling in time to prune evergreen shrubs, reminders to protect delicate plants from forthcoming frosts, or notes on the best time to sow herbs or wild flower seeds, recording seasonal tasks will help ensure that your garden performs at its best all year round.

Over time, this written record will become an invaluable resource you can turn to year on year.

JANUARY

Week 1

Week 2

Week 3

Week 4

Week 5

FEBRUARY

Week 1

Week 2

Week 3

Week 4

Week 5

MARCH

Week 1

Week 2

Week 3

Week 4

Week 5

APRIL

Week 1

Week 2

Week 3

Week 4

Week 5

MAY

Week 1

Week 2

Week 3

Week 4

Week 5

JUNE

Week 1

Week 2

Week 3

Week 4

Week 5

JULY

Week 1

Week 2

Week 3

Week 4

Week 5

AUGUST

Week 1

Week 2

Week 3

Week 4

Week 5

SEPTEMBER

Week 1

Week 2

Week 3

Week 4

Week 5

OCTOBER

Week 1

Week 2

Week 3

Week 4

Week 5

NOVEMBER

Week 1

Week 2

Week 3

Week 4

Week 5

DECEMBER

Week 1

Week 2

Week 3

Week 4

Week 5

notes

useful contacts

Name:

Address:

Tel:

Email:

www.

Comments:

Name:

Address:

Tel:

Email:

www.

Comments:

Name:

Address:

Tel:

Email:

www.

Comments:

Name:

Address:

Tel:

Email:

www.

Comments:

Name:

Address:

Tel:

Email:

www.

Comments:

Name:

Address:

Tel:

Email:

www.

Comments:

favorite stores

Name:

Address:

Tel:

Email:

www.

Comments:

Name:

Address:

Tel:

Email:

www.

Comments:

Name:

Address:

Tel:

Email:

www.

Comments:

Name:

Address:

Tel:

Email:

www.

Comments:

Name:

Address:

Tel:

Email:

www.

Comments:

Name:

Address:

Tel:

Email:

www.

Comments:

picture credits

Key = a=above, b=below, r=right, l=left

Jan Baldwin 47
Peter Cassidy 105
Helen Cathcart 43
Christopher Drake 53
Tara Fisher 20, 61, 70, 80
Michelle Garrett 35
Georgia Glynn-Smith 32
Winfried Heinze 115
Anne Hyde 50
Nick Ivins 44

Gavin Kingcome 1, 2, 4, 17, 19, 41, 42, 66, 73,
Kim Lightbody 18
David Merewether 7, 59, 60, 62, 65, 69, 76, 79,
88r, 89, 93, 99, 103, 104, 106, 109, 113
Emma Mitchell 3, 26
Martin Norris /Emma Mitchell 6, 26
Keiko Oikawa/Amanda Darcy 74
Debbie Patterson 5, 29
Heini Schneebeli 114
Lucinda Symons 87l, 90
Polly Wreford 23